Journalling for Scrapbookers

Simple formulas to transform your scrapbooks from photo albums to precious books..

Go from worried writer to journalling pro

Linda Gransby

Acknowledgments

To my editor Maggie

Your encouragement and enthusiasm for my ideas has spurred me on to complete my second book. And for your regular sanity checks, I thank you!

To my weekend retreat ladies

I'd like to give massive and heartfelt appreciation to all my craft retreat ladies for being my 'guinea pigs' for the ideas and concepts for this book.

To my book reviewers

Thank you for taking the time to leave a review on Amazon, I really appreciate it.

In this book

Welcome!

I'm really excited to bring you my latest book - Journalling for Scrapbookers.

Have you've ever sat at your craft table staring at a page, and you really don't want to write on it in case you spoil it?

Do you put off writing anything on your scrapbook pages because you just don't know where to start?

I hear people all the time at my retreats, talking about how they struggle with what to write on their pages. How to start and what to say. Writing interesting and compelling memories for the reader of the album, becomes a chore.

I'm here to change that. I'm going to show you how to enjoy, and even look forward to journalling in your albums.

There something very special about being given a book that has been made especially for you and your life.

Let me help you make wonderful books full of precious memories that your family and friends will love to read.

Linda x

Create an album to remember

Making scrapbook albums of your photos is wonderful, but without the writing to tell the story, your readers are missing out on the experience of hearing about the event or person:

Little things that happened or a baby's first experiences of the seaside that you can't glean from a photo.

What about the family's weird Christmas traditions or why you always pick the same spot on the beach on your summer holiday?

These memories, combined with the photos, will add up to a scrapbook that will be valued and cherished for many years by family and friends.

How this book will help

This book will help you transform your scrapbooks from photo albums to precious books that will make your loved ones laugh, cry and enjoy precious memories with you.

Your guide to stress free journalling

```
Journal|Journalling
  \Jur • nal\n\v\adj

To write about events,
people or thoughts;
travel notes; to keep a
diary
```

Creating your album pages is wonderful, reliving the moments, adding the beautiful papers, stickers and embellishments.

But its only half the story....

Our album readers miss out on the full experience because we don't write on our pages.

- Do you put off writing on your pages?
- Think you are bad at spelling?
- Don't know what to write?
- Worried about spoiling your pages with your handwriting?

You're not alone....

Help is here!

I've put together some simple tips and techniques that will take you from worried writer to journalling pro.

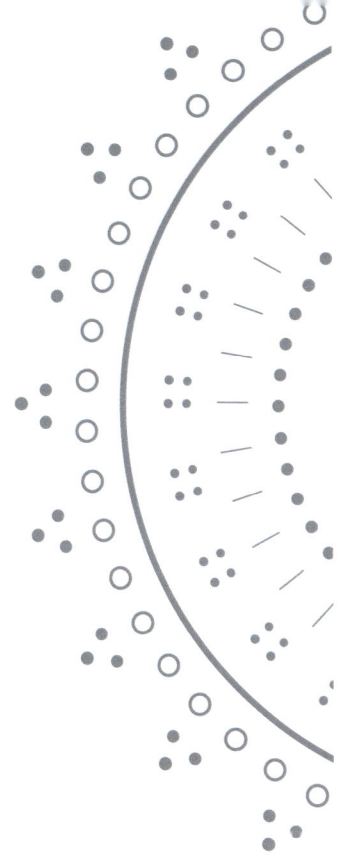

Getting started

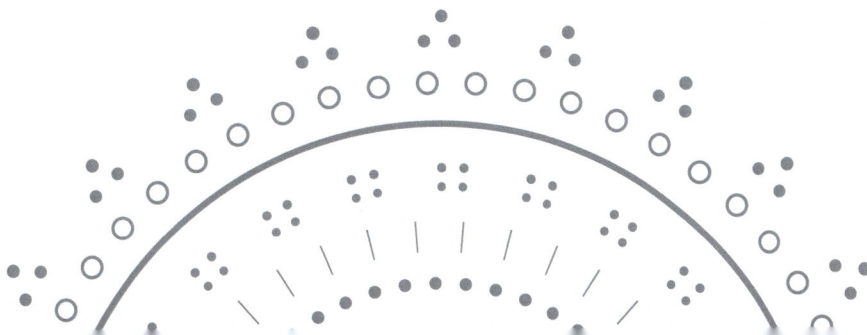

Video summary

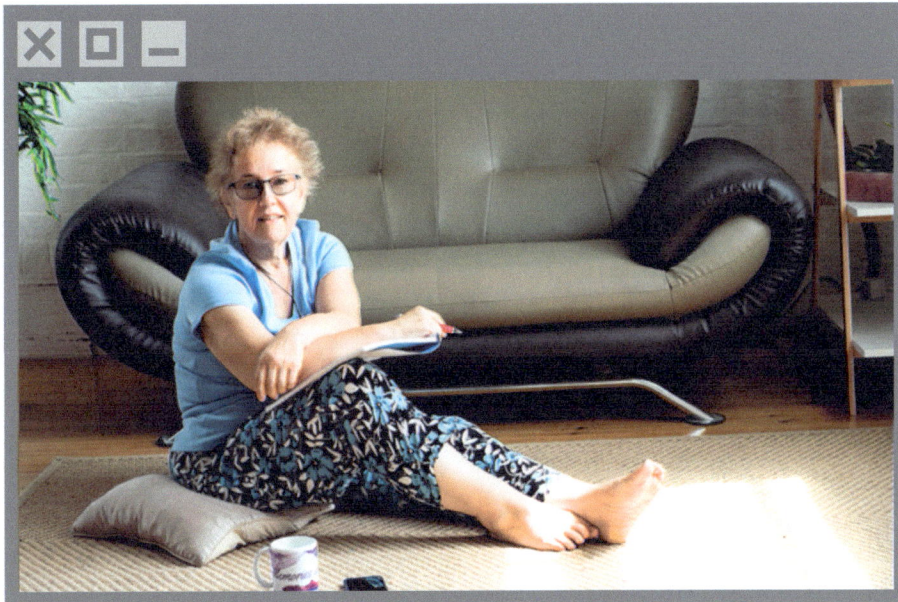

Want a quick video summary that will help you get started on your journalling quickly?

Check out this video overview of how to get started

In this short video I cover 3 things:

What's your why?

Basic supplies you'll need to get started
(hint - its not much)

How to use the book

To play the video:
click below or type this link into your browser
memoriesandphotos.co.uk/pages/free-resources

Don't skimp the ink

How long do you want your journalling to last on the page?

As scrapbookers we spend many happy and creative hours making pages for our families, our friends and ourselves.

The type of pen you use is as important as using the right glue for your photos.

Permanent ink gives your writing the best chance of still being readable 50 years or 100 years from now.

It won't smuge or run if your album gets damp, and it won't fade in the light.

Beware!

- Don't use biro ink, its not photo safe and will spoil your photos

- Don't use ink on the back of your photos - save if for the journalling

- Do - use a soft pencil to label the reverse of your photos

What do I need to get started?

You have what you need already, I guarantee it....

- A pen or pencil
- A notebook
- A mug of tea or coffee
- Five minutes without interruptions

Ok, there is one more thing....

Lets not complicate things. You don't need a calligraphy pen, (unless you're already proficient with one)

When you want to write in your album I would suggest you get a permanent ink marker pen.

These cost very little and will ensure that the words you write don't fade or get smudged by moisture.

I recommend the UniPin black permanent pen.

They are available in different nib sizes, my preference for writing is 0.8mm. You can buy them from stationary and art shops.

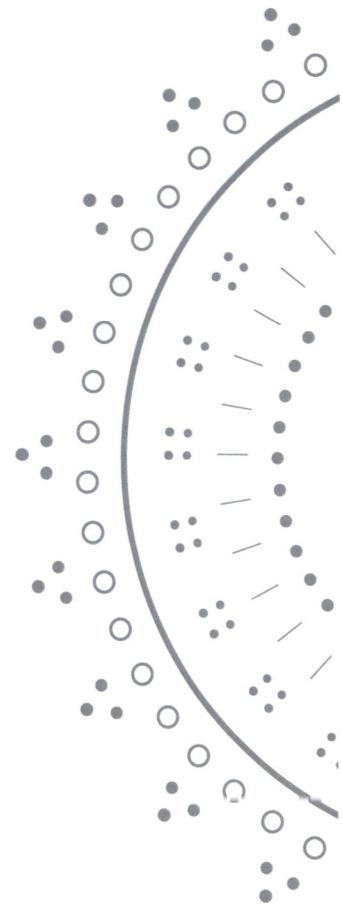

Journalling Formulas

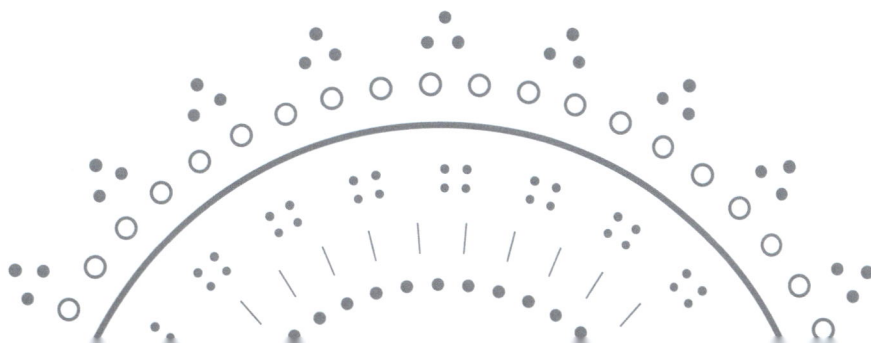

Three journalling formulas to use

I know a lot of people find journaling difficult, and put off doing it (me included) Some people enjoy writing more than others, and thats ok. But everyone CAN do it.

The good news is like any other skill you can learn how to do it, and you will improve with practice.

Writing about the memories will give your scrapbooks a depth and lasting importance that will make them treasured heirlooms.

You have something unique and valuable to say on pages that will make them precious and memorable to your family and friends.

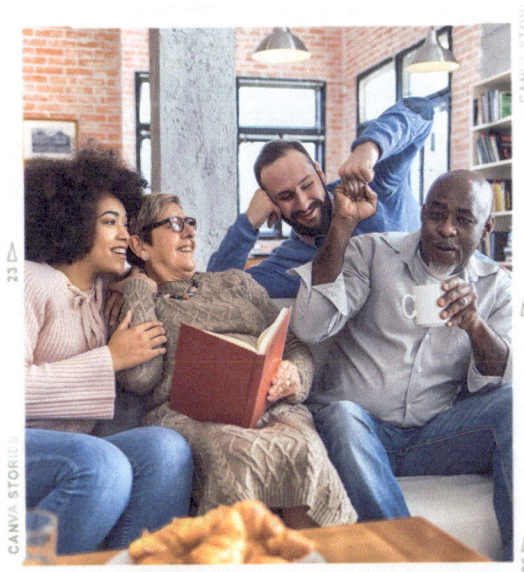

The knack is knowing how to get what you have inside of you into a written form.

On the next pages are 3 ways to get your journalling flowing effortlessly.

Technique 1 - The five 'W's journalling

At the very least, you should always include some of the 5 W's on your pages...

1. Who
2. What
3. Where
4. When
5. Why

1. Who is in the photo?

Names and a date on your pages are especially important. You don't have to label every page in an album, but it's important to make it clear who the main characters are and when the photos were taken.

This might not seem important now, but in 20 or 50 years it will be. If you are not around to explain, would the people looking at this picture know who it is?

Also remember that people change over the years, children look very different as adults, and babies all look very alike, so naming is important.

- Names of people in the photos (not just mum, grandpa)
- If the same people feature a lot, use first and last names somewhere in the album, doesn't have to be every photo
- If not family, mention the person's relationship to the family: friend, work colleagues etc.

Linda's Tip: Use a summary page at the front of a family album, with pictures and names of all the people featured in the book

If I were to create a scrapbook page about this photo using the name and date journaling approach, I would simply include a line that said something like :

'Karen and John with Ethan and Lily,
May 2017'.

This would be the minimum you write on a page....it's a start.

Make sure you are including names of those pictured several times within an album or each time someone new is introduced

Try and include the full family name at least once or twice too.

2. When was it taken?

Adding a day, month and year gives the photographs context and allows the view to compare different years activities.

Historically its also very interesting to see how clothing and hair styles looked, for instance, in the 1990s, compared to present day.

You could add further context by talking about notable events in the year your photos were taken, what the people in them were experiencing in the 'real world' around them makes interesting reading and adds insight to their lives.

Try:
- Date
- Day
- Month
- Year
- Notable events in history at that time
- Notable events in your family at that time (that you may not have photos for)
- Monetary value of things in that particular year

3. Where was the photo taken?

Background information about the place in the photos adds interest and history.

Even talking about the family house at the time, where it is, what room the people are in and quirky things about the house.

What the town or street you lived in was like.

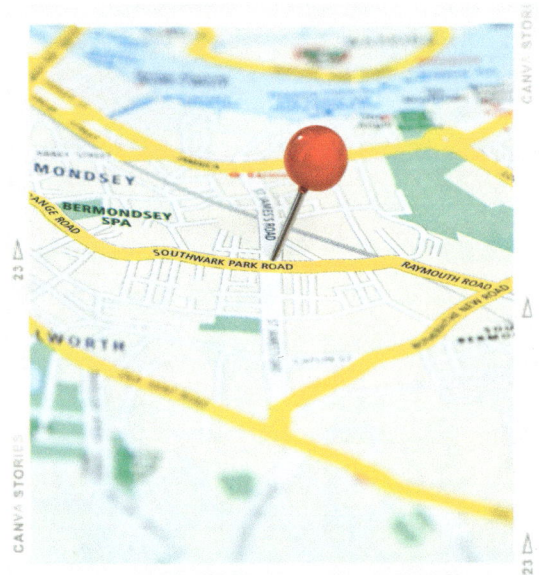

Try:
- Where is the location of the photo?
- Home, work, friend's house, club?
- House address, name of church wedding was held etc.
- Country and town

4 & 5. What is the event, why is this going on?

People like to read about what the photos were about.

Maybe a family party, summer barbeque, work reunion, baptism etc.

Include details about what happened on the day, anything memorable that happened that there's no photo for.

Try:
- What event was being photographed?
- Why did you take the photos?
- Why is the event happening?
- Describe memorable moments?
- What did you enjoy most about the event/ what did relatives say?

Technique 2 - Standing over the shoulder journalling

Imagine someone is sitting down and looking at an album you made, and you are right there with them standing by their shoulder.

They say, "how cute!" or "I love that photo!" or something to that effect. What do you say in return? Do you just say "thanks" and then turn the page?

More likely you would tell them something more about the photo, the page, or a funny story that is related to what you are looking at. That is exactly what you should write down!

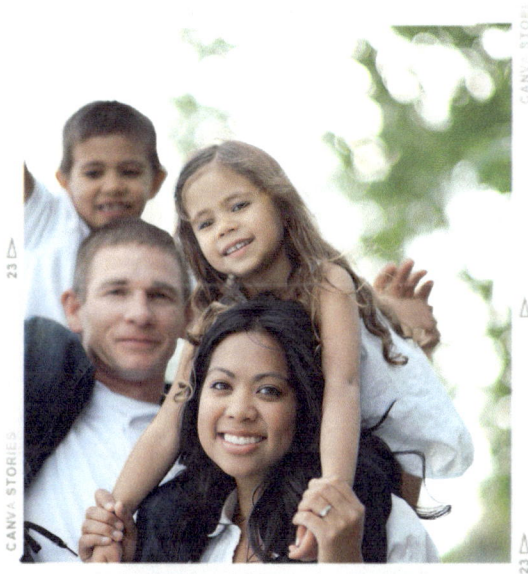

Let's look at the original photo again.

If I were journalling about this image using this technique, I might write something like

'This photo was taken in our favourite spot in the garden just after we found out Karen was pregnant again'.

You might not always be there to explain what was happening in a photo or why you chose to scrapbook that memory, but you can explain on the page using this technique. This approach works for almost any type of page.

Try:
- Imagine you are showing someone your page
- What hidden story would you tell them about the pictures
- Jot it down, use it to journal your page

Technique 3 - Surprise your reader

This is when you really get into the details. We're going beyond stating the obvious about your pictures. Forget 'Our family at the seaside, we can see that already!

This time, do you have a piece of information that will really surprise them?

Can you think of something interesting that only those who are in the photo would know?

Is something happening outside the edge of the photo?

Does this moment bring back other memories?

Let's look at the original photo once more.

If I were to create a scrapbook page about this photo using the surprise your reader approach, I would tell the viewer some fun details that would change the way they look at this photo.

For instance, 'Ten seconds after this photo was taken, Ethan kicked John in the face and gave him a black eye!' or 'This reminds me of the special corner of the garden where we planted our wedding tree; each year we measure the children's height against it'

Don't you feel much more interested in the photo now that you know the story behind it?

Try:
- What is the hidden story behind the photo?
- Personal stories that start – do you remember when......?
- What's happening outside the frame of the photo that we can't see?
- Interesting things that only the people that were there would know.

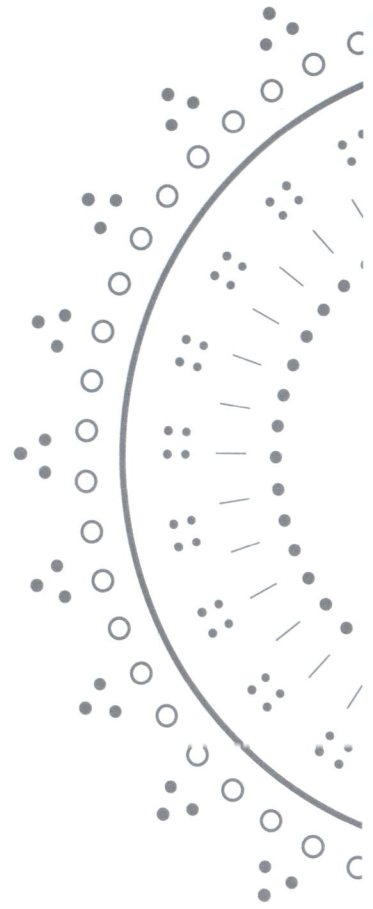

Quick Tips

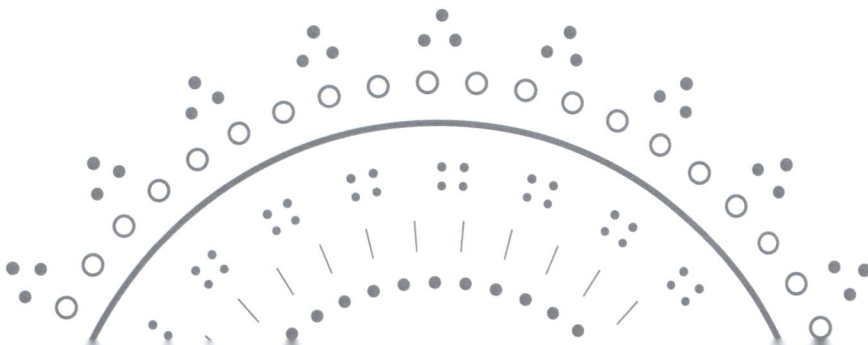

10 Quick tips

Use a pen labelled as permanent so your journalling doesn't fade.

Write each person's full name at least one place in each album (your future readers won't know who 'mum' is.

If you are short of time or inspiration, the least journalling on each page should be name, date and place or event.

Write on cardstock and stick it to your page. It takes the pressure off, and if you make a mistake, you've not spoilt the page.

Add hidden journalling in a mini envelope stuck to your page.

10 Quick tips

6 Get a relative talking about memories by taking along something that will trigger memories.

7 Don't be afraid of handwriting, even if you think its untidy. It's what makes your album personal.

8 Make a list instead of using sentences. (10 memorable moments about the day, etc).

9 Take a photo of place names, maps etc. They will help you remember when you journal.

10 Carry a small notebook in your bag to jot down memorable moments before you forget them.

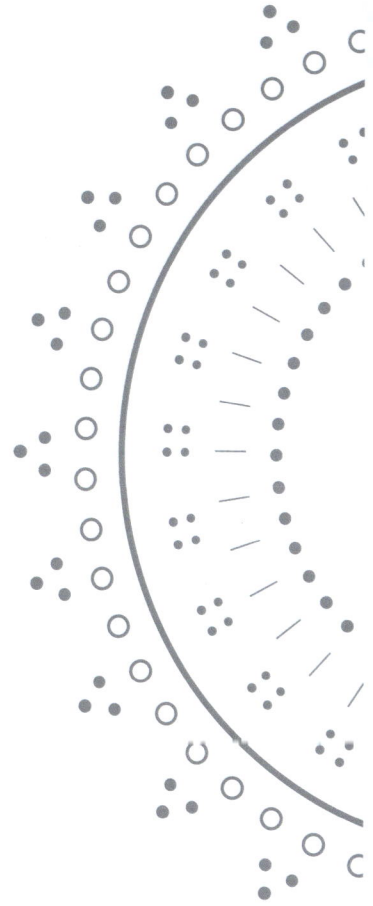

Solving Worries

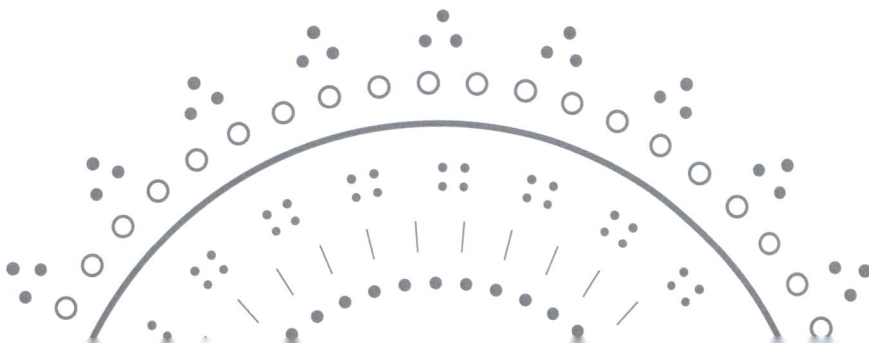

Worries that might stop you starting

I don't like my handwriting

Your readers are not expecting calligraphy, they are more interested in the story than whether you have written neatly….

Your handwriting is a unique part of you and connects you to your reader.

When you get a hand addressed envelope in the post at Christmas, have you ever played the 'guess who this is from' game?

That because our writing is distinct to us, it invokes memories in our families and friends.

Make your album unique, add a bit of 'you' to each page!

What if I spoil my page with my handwriting?

See the above answer!

You're not spoiling your page; you are connecting with your family and friends.

They will enjoy a hand written album more than perfect computer printed journalling, its more personal

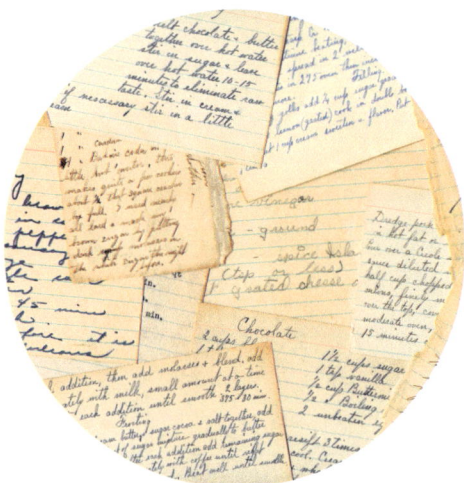

Worries that might stop you starting

What if I make a mistake?

I've been there...... You've made a layout to be proud of, and you're worried you'll muck up the writing.

Try these suggestions

- Write out what you want to say in rough first
- Check spelling
- Make sure your pen is working well
- Its paper – you can always stick something over the mistake and start again
- Do your journalling on a loose piece of cardstock or paper and then glue it in. Make a mistake, start again

I havent got time!

- Journalling doesn't have to take loads of time.

- Not all layouts need paragraphs of prose

- Use bullet points for quick journalling

- Carry a notebook and use time while waiting for appointments, kids etc to jot down notes.

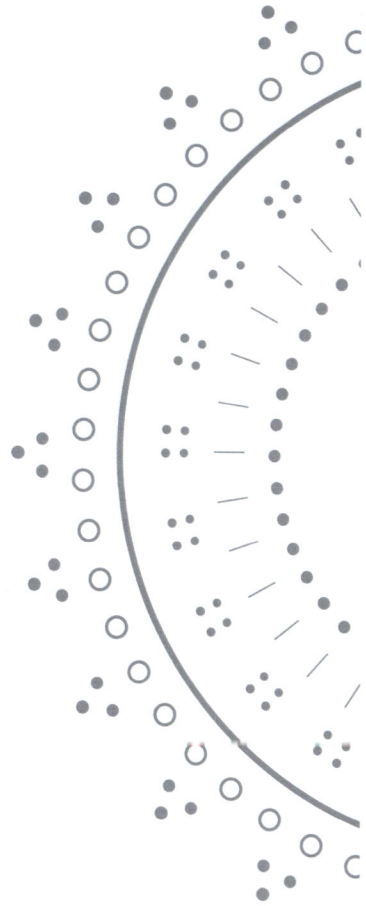

Quick ideas to get you unstuck

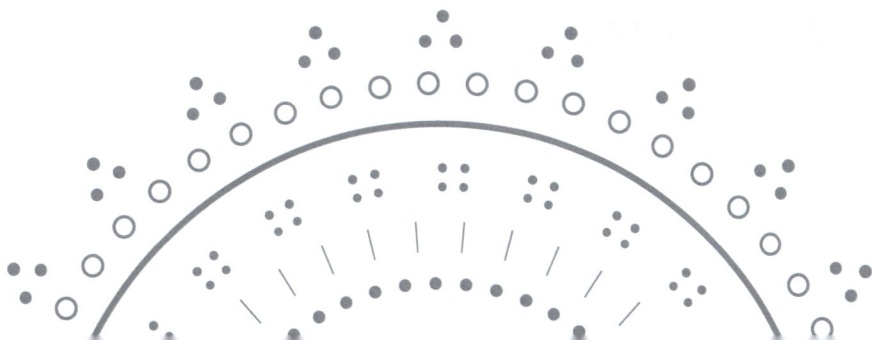

Ideas to get you unstuck

Just start writing, go with the flow
Grab some paper and start writing anything, shopping list, song lyrics, copy something from a magazine or book.

The sheer act of writing will get your brain in the right mode.

Write down what you know
Pick a layout, and start writing everything you know about that particular place, event, people etc.

Doing this helps your subconscious brain connect with other related memories connected to the layout. Think about stories of the day you can tell someone who wasn't there.

Use an idea notebook
Carrying a notebook is a great way to start your journalling before you even get started on the page.

Writing memories while you are still 'in the moment' means you'll capture far more than if you try to remember later. (Try remembering your child's first words when you make their baby album five years later!)

It's equally important if you are travelling, so you can note down place names and what you did each day. It's surprising how quickly you can forget what you did yesterday!

Write badly
Grab some scrap paper and just write. Don't judge grammar, spellings or how neat it is. Just get your brain into writing mode. You can tidy it up later.

Ideas to get you unstuck

Write a letter to your readers
Write a letter to someone about your layout. Tell them all about what's in the photos, then add it to your page.

Don't forget to add 'Dear' and 'love from'

Use quotes, song lyrics, poems
Do the photos on your page remind you of a particular song, or quote.

You could use this for your journalling. Remember to also include the five 'W's' too.

Speak your writing
Use a dictation app on your electronic device and just talk your journalling. You'll get a more authentic 'voice' that reflects you.

You can edit it later. Try the app 'Otter' on your phone, or check what you've already got on your PC, you might have one built-in already

Try using a different style
Sports day pictures could be written as a newspaper report. A holiday could have a review of the hotel. Garden pictures could be written as a brochure for seeds. Think creatively.

Leave a gap
I work better at journalling if I do it all in one go. I leave a gap on each page for my writing, then make time at the end of the day or weekend to add my thoughts.

Ideas to get you unstuck

Make a list
10 memorable moments, 7 things I enjoyed, 5 places to visit.... Etc etc

Get others to do the journalling
Take cardstock and pens to events and get people to write something about the day to add to your pages.

Collect information as you go
Relevant brochures, train or plane tickets, magazines, newspaper articles can all act as sources of information. They'll also act as a memory jogger when you get around to the writing.

Interview someone
Ask someone who was at the event you are scrapbooking for their memories of the day. What was their favourite moment, what did they enjoy, funny things that happened.

Memorobilia Memory joggers
Don't forget to gather physical mementos like brochures, tickets, and articles that will help you recall the details of each moment. These items will not only add depth to your pages but will also serve as prompts for your writing.

Remember that there is no one "right way" to document your memories. Just focus on including the information that will make your pages lasting and meaningful.

A freebie for you

FREE

I've made a scrapbook page planner sheet to help you save time working out your pages

It has sections on

- colour wheel
- layout sketch area
- journalling notes
- supplies tick list
- photo notes

To get yours, just click here, or scan the QR code below with your device:

bit.ly/sbpageplannersheet

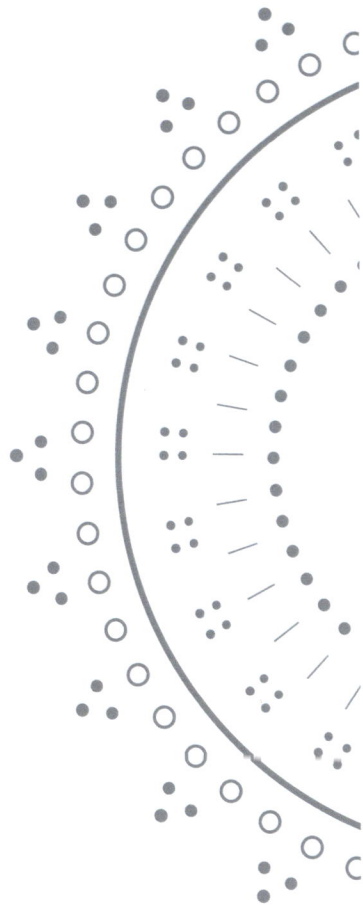

In depth - more formulas

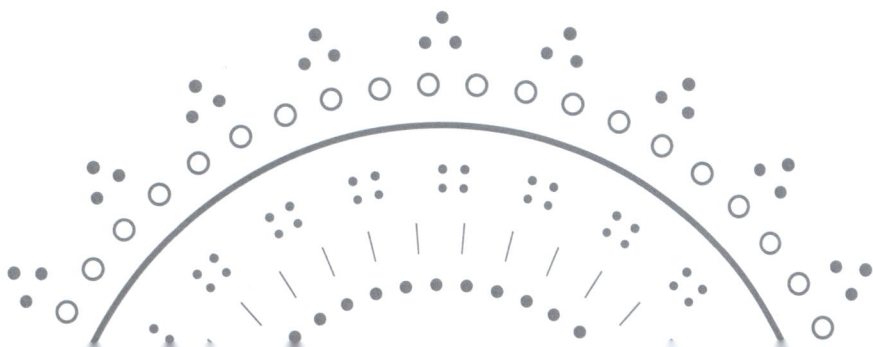

More techniques - Freewriting

Freewriting is a writing technique that involves generating spontaneous and uninterrupted flow of thoughts on paper or a digital document.

The key characteristic of freewriting is that you write without worrying about grammar, structure, or coherence.

The goal is to let your thoughts flow freely and uninhibited, which frees up your subconscious mind, and overcomes writers block.

Freewriting allows your subconscious mind to express itself, and by letting your thoughts flow without constraints, you can tap into your creative potential.

This method encourages a state of flow, where you become absorbed in the act of writing without thinking, and ideas come more naturally.

Advantages of this method

This style of generating journaling is a liberating and emotionally charged form of writing that prioritizes the authentic expression of feelings and thoughts.

With practice, you can create open and free-flowing writing, allowing emotions to guide the pen without the constraints of a structured format.

It serves as a powerful tool for emotional honesty, and can provide an outlet for you to release and process pent-up emotions.

This exploits the therapeutic value of unfiltered self-expression, fostering a sense of authenticity, and emotional honesty in your journalling.

More techniques - Freewriting

Here's how to give it a go:

- Decide on a duration. It could be 5, 10, or 15 minutes.

- Grab a rough notebook and pen, or you favourite digital note taking app.

- As we are doing this for scrapbooking, choose the photos you'll be scrapbooking, or the completed pages that need journalling added.

- Begin writing whatever comes to your mind. Don't worry about spelling, grammar, or punctuation.

- Write continuously without stopping.

- Don't go back and make corrections. The focus is on generating ideas without self-censorship.

- Ideally, turn off auto correct if you are using a digital notetaking app.

- If you get stuck, continue writing the last word or phrase until a new idea comes to mind.

- Let your thoughts flow from one to another, writing down as you go, even if it takes you off on a tangent.

- This process frees up the creative side of your brain, and triggers memories.

- After the allotted time, review what you've written. At this point you can edit and refine.

More techniques - Memory maps

Bearing in mind that if you a reading this, you are probably a 'creative' person... A memory map is a graphical representation of your memories, rather than a linear one.

You start off with a central theme, and then add ideas which radiate out as branches. You can use different pens, and colour too.

Drawing your notes in this unlocks the creative (right) side of your brain, and is proven to increase memory recall, compared to paragraphs of writing which is interpreted by the logical (left) side of your brain.

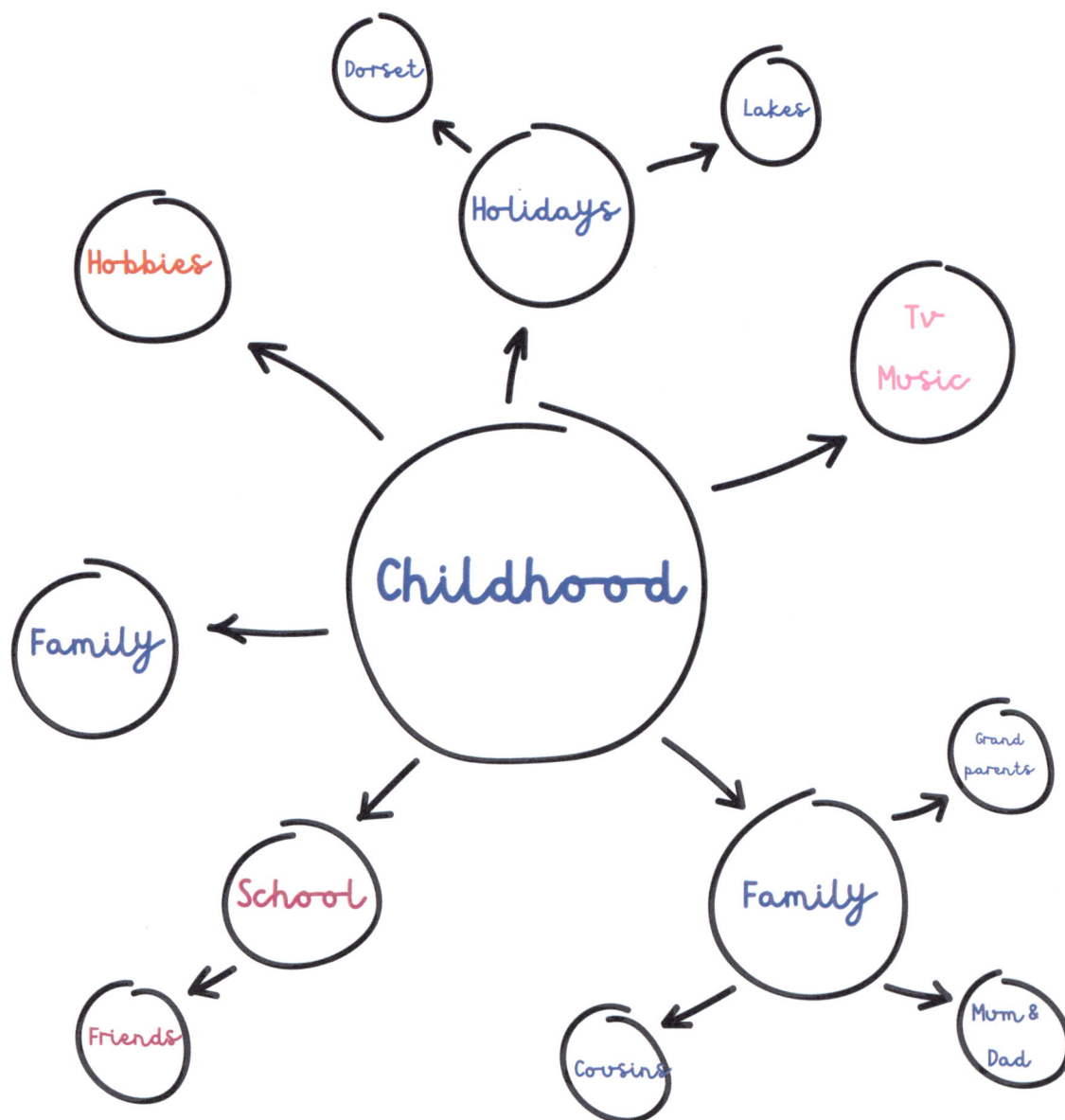

More techniques - Memory maps

Here's **how to get started:**

- Grab some rough paper, A4 or letter is a good size to start with.

- Decide which of your layouts you're going to 'Memory Map'.

- Write the main theme in the centre of your page and circle it.

- From the central point, create branches representing different categories or sub-themes related to your memories. E.g. if your central theme is "Childhood," branches could include "Family," "School," "Friends,".

- Extend each branch with more specific details. Use keywords, short phrases, or even small sketches to represent these details.

- Try colours, symbols, and doodles to distinguish between various elements or emotions.

- You can revisit your rough copy to refine it, and then either draw a new version for your album or use the memory map as a basis for more extensive journalling.

More techniques - Narrative Style

Imagine being the narrator of a film or book. It's you telling a story in the first-person past tense, through words that complement the visual photos on your page. This creates a more immersive and engaging experience for you and your readers.

Begin your journalling by setting the scene. Describe the background of the photos, the emotions captured, and the significance of the moment. This helps create a context for the images on the page.

E.g. "On a warm summer afternoon at Grandma's backyard, laughter echoed as we gathered for a family reunion. The sun warmed us, and the delicious smell of barbecued burgers filled the air."

Delve into the emotions felt during those moments. Share your thoughts, feelings, and reactions to the people and activities captured in the photos.

E.g. "I was so happy as I watched the kids play together, their laughter echoing around the garden. It was a reminder of the precious bond we share as a family."

Paint a vivid picture with your words. Use descriptive language to bring your memories to life. Appeal to the senses by incorporating details about colours, textures, sounds, and scents.

E.g. "The vibrant hues of the autumn leaves surrounded us, crunching beneath our feet as we strolled through the park. The crisp air carried the sound of ducks quacking on the pond, and the distant sound of a commuter train."

More techniques - Narrative Style

Share interesting anecdotes or specific moments that may not be evident in the photos alone.

E.g "As we huddled around the campfire, exchanging stories and roasting marshmallows, Aunt Martha shared a hilarious tale from her youth, leaving us in stitches. It was a night filled with laughter, warmth, and the timeless joy of family bonding."

Organize your journaling in a way that creates a natural flow. Consider the chronological order of events or group similar memories together. This helps the reader follow the narrative seamlessly.

E.g. "From the first tentative steps on the hiking trail to the summit photos, our mountain adventure unfolded. Each snapshot capturing a different chapter of our journey."

You could conclude your narration with personal reflections from the experience or a message to your readers.

E.g. "As I look back at these photos, I'm reminded that it's not just about the places we go or the things we do; it's about the shared moments and laughter with people we love.

More techniques - Bullet points

When you're not sure where to start or are dealing with a multitude of thoughts, bullet points can serve as a brainstorming tool.

You can jot down ideas quickly without worrying about the structure. You can either use them as they are or expand on each point into a fuller form of journalling.

Simplicity

This method is clear and concise, and the simplicity can free up your mind, allowing for more creative expression.

Using them encourages a flow of ideas that might be stifled by more traditional paragraph-style writing.

Bullet points make your journal entries concise and easy to read. It allows the reader to quickly scan and understand the key points and prevents your writing from becoming too wordy.

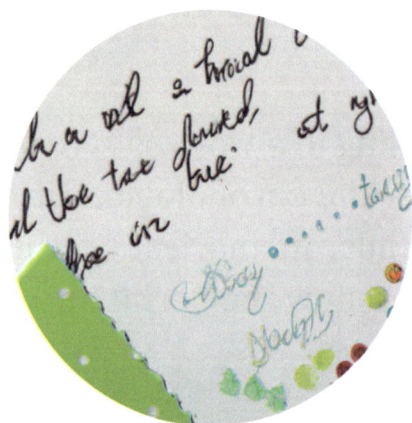

Time saving

They enable you to record your thoughts quickly, allowing you to capture the journalling when you have very little time.

It's easier to reflect on specific aspects of the event or emotions. You can create lists of things you're grateful for, achievements, challenges, or any other elements you want to reflect on.

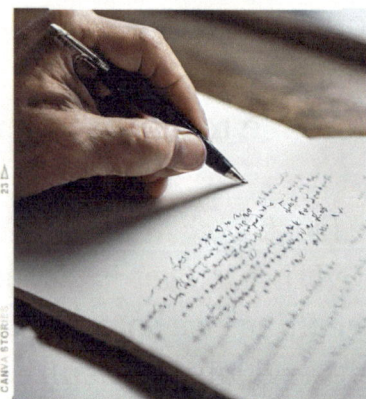

More techniques - Bullet points

Here's a bullet point list (!) of things to try:

- List key moments or highlights from the photos.
- Places visited or lived in.
- Jobs or places worked.
- Favourite foods from your trip.
- List names and roles of people featured in the images.
- Outline the main locations.
- Highlight specific objects, symbols, or details.
- Note any important dates.
- List of significant milestones.
- Write a list of memorable moments for your page.
- List the emotions or reactions captured in the photos.
- Create a bullet point timeline of events.
- Include a list of personal reflections or insights.
- Your bucket list items.
- What happened in a particular month/year.

More techniques - Storytelling

Start with thinking about the story you want to convey on the page.

Think about writing an introduction, a middle with the main story of what happened, and an ending or conclusion to the story

Experimenting with first-person, second-person, and third-person narratives

First Person

Write a narrative of the chosen story in the first person. Use "I" and "we" pronouns to convey a personal perspective. Share your thoughts, feelings, and experiences related to the story.

Second Person

Rewrite the narrative using second person pronouns ("you" and "your"). This involves addressing the reader directly, allowing them to step into the shoes of the person experiencing the story.

Third Person

Transform the narrative once again, this time using third person pronouns ("he," "she," "they"). Depict the story as an observer, providing a more detached perspective.

More techniques - Storytelling

Here's how to get started

- Describe the lead up to the main event or moment captured in the photos. These could be milestones, emotions, or significant experiences.

- Start your page with an introduction that sets the stage for the narrative. Include details like the date, location, and any relevant background information.

- Explain why this particular moment was important or memorable.

- Share any surprising or unexpected twists that occurred during the event.

- Highlight the key people involved and their roles in the story. Make sure you name them and explain who they are if its the first time they feature in your album.

- Reflect on how this moment impacted your life. Include memories that capture the essence of each moment. Share your thoughts, feelings, and reflections

- Discuss any problems challenges or obstacles you overcame.

- Compare this event to similar ones from your past.

- Describe your thoughts and feelings leading up to the moment.

- Share your hopes and dreams related to the future.

- Consider the impact of the event, or decisions that you made.

- Organize the key moments in chronological order to create a cohesive and natural flow. This will help readers follow the story seamlessly.

- Conclude your pages with a thoughtful reflection or summary.

More techniques - Top tens

Writing down your top 10 memories or observations on scrapbook pages is a really quick and easy way to do journalling, without the stress of creative writing expectations hanging over you.

Top ten lists provide a structured format, helping to organize your thoughts in a clear and concise manner. This can make your journal entries easier to read and understand.

Crafting a limited list of 10 requires you to think about what is most important or relevant, bringing focus to your journaling.

Creating lists can stimulate your creativity. It encourages you to think outside the box and come up with different ideas or solutions within a defined structure.

More techniques - Top tens

Here's a few suggestions:

- Create a list related to the photos on the page.
- List the events of the day depicted on your pages.
- Make a list of the places featured in the photos.
- List the things I love about the people featured in the images.
- Compile a list of adventures or journeys associated with the photos.
- Create a family traditions list if the photos capture special family moments.
- A list of the events 10 highlights / lowlights.
- A list of 10 quotes from people in the photos.
- Write down a list of who is featured in the photos.
- Memorable places.
- Memorable moments.
- Top 10 holidays.
- 10 favourites.

More techniques - Lyrics, poems and quotes

If you are struggling what to say on your pages, why not use someone else's words!

There are many quote and lyric sites online that you can search for free.

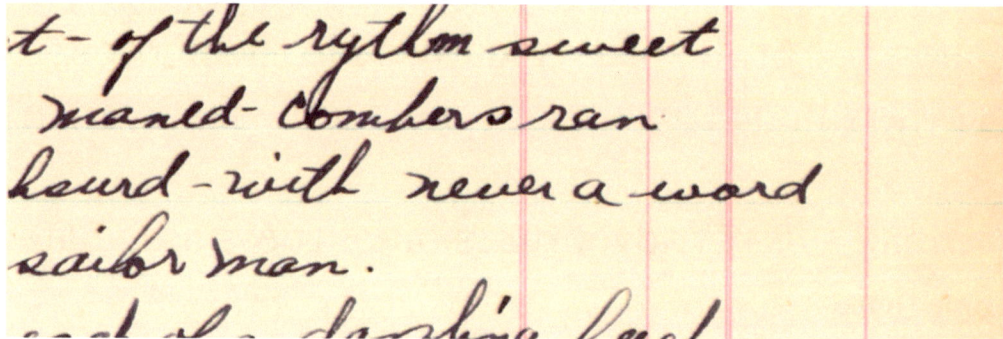

Use the experts

Using quotes, poems, or lyrics in your scrapbook journaling can enrich the overall experience and providing a unique touch to your creative project.

This method can convey emotions and sentiments that you might find challenging to express in your own words.

Save time struggling.

Selecting quotes, poems, or lyrics that resonate with you personally allows you to infuse your emotions on the page without spending lots of time struggling to find the right words.

Quotes or lyrics from songs that were popular during a specific time can act as a nostalgic reminder, capturing the essence of a particular period in your life.

More techniques - Lyrics, poems and quotes

Try these:

- Find a meaningful quote or song lyric that complements the theme of the page.
- Consider quotes from literature, movies, or even personal conversations that hold significant meaning.
- Explain why you chose the words and how they relate to the photos.
- Write about a personal connection you have to the words in the quote.
- Google search for song lyrics that capture the essence of the photos.
- Describe how the lyrics resonate with you.
- Share any memories or stories related to the source of the quote.
- Explain what the quote, saying or lyrics mean to you.
- Reflect on how the quote has inspired or motivated you.

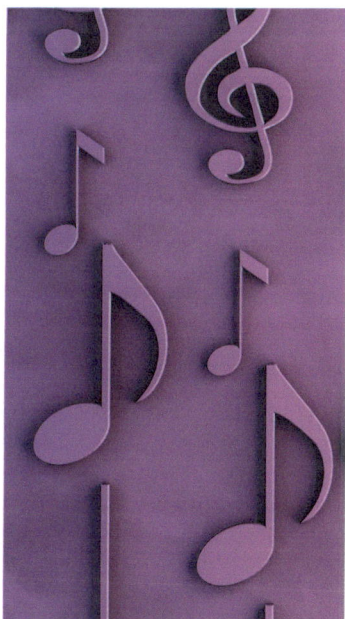

Linda's tip:

Create music playlists to use when you are scrapbooking and journalling.

Curate music to match different moods, for instance energetic, creative, or relaxed

More techniques - Letters and correspondence

In this digital age, where communication often happens in the blink of an eye, there's something magical about handwritten letters.

They carry a personal touch and timeless appeal that can't be replicated by emails or text messages. Scrapbooking, with its emphasis on preserving memories and capturing moments, provides the perfect canvas for incorporating letter writing.

Embrace the authenticity and imperfection inherent in handwritten correspondence.

Unlike digital communication, where autocorrect and editing tools can polish every word, handwritten letters have a raw and genuine quality that speaks to the heart.

Don't worry about achieving perfection in your writing; instead, focus on vulnerability, and sincerity. Allow your handwriting to reflect the ebb and flow of emotions, creating an intimate connection between you and the reader

Using letters as a form of journaling in your scrapbooking is a creative and personal way to document your thoughts, feelings, and memories.

Think of it as writing a letter to your future self, or to the person in the photos, sharing thoughts, advice, or wishes.

Consider writing letters to your children, grandchildren, or loved ones, sharing family stories, traditions, and values

More techniques - Letters and correspondence

Here are some ideas on how to incorporate letter writing into your scrapbooking:

Personal Letters

Write letters to yourself or to someone else. Express your thoughts, emotions, and reflections on the events or experiences captured in the scrapbook. Include the letters on separate pages or alongside related photos and embellishments.

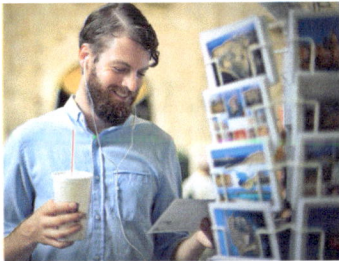

Postcards

Collect postcards when you travel and write about your day on each one. Post them back to yourself, and include them in your holiday album.

Timeline Letters

Write letters as if you were communicating with your future self or someone from the past. Reflect on where you are in life at that moment. Date the letters, creating a timeline of your experiences.

Theme-Based Letters

Choose a specific theme for your scrapbook page, and write a letter related to that theme. For example, if your scrapbook is about a trip, write a letter detailing your favourite moments and discoveries.

Hidden Letters

Write letters on separate pieces of paper and tuck them into pockets, envelopes, or behind photos. Include hints or labels on the page to guide readers to the hidden letters or leave them secret, just for you.

Linda's Tip:

Attach small pockets to your pages to hold keepsakes like letters, and postcards

More techniques - Dialogue

Create a conversation between the people in the photos or have them "speak" about the moment captured.

Dialogues can make your journal entries feel more personal and engaging. By capturing conversations, you bring readers into the moment, allowing them to connect with the emotions and experiences you're describing.

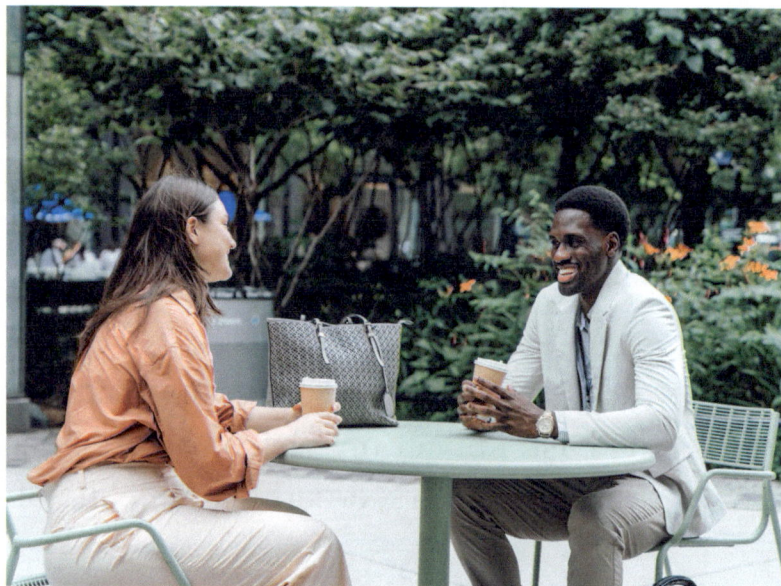

This technique adds a sense of realism to your storytelling. Replicate the way people actually speak, making your entries more authentic and relatable. This can help convey the genuine emotions and atmosphere of a particular moment.

Dialogues provide an opportunity for character development. You can showcase personalities, relationships, and the dynamics between individuals through the way they speak and interact.

Dialogue can make your journal entries more dynamic. It breaks up long paragraphs of narration and can create a faster-paced, engaging read. This is especially beneficial if you want your scrapbook to be lively and captivating.

More techniques - Dialogue

If your scrapbook involves multiple people or viewpoints, dialogue allows you to convey different perspectives. You can include the voices of others, providing a more well-rounded and comprehensive view of an event or experience.

By recording dialogues, you're preserving the essence of those moments, capturing what was said can trigger vivid memories for your reader.

Here's a few ideas to try

- Create a dialogue between people in the photos, allowing them to "speak" about the moment.

- Imagine a conversation between yourself and someone else in the images.

- Write a playful or humorous dialogue to lighten the tone of the page.

- Explore the thoughts and feelings of the individuals in the photos through their conversation.

- Use dialogue to share anecdotes, inside jokes, or shared memories.

- Incorporate fictional dialogue that adds a creative twist to the narrative.

- Use dialogue to share anecdotes, inside jokes, or shared memories.

- Incorporate fictional dialogue that adds a creative twist to the narrative.

- Express the hopes and dreams of the people in the images through their conversation.

- Use dialogue to convey the essence of the relationships depicted in the photos.

More techniques - Interviews

If you are struggling to write the memories on your pages, think about asking other people to help.

You'll get a different perspective to you own view and it will spark your creativity too. Interview the people in the photos and include their thoughts and memories in your journaling.

Connection and authenticity

Interviews provide a direct connection to the people involved in the events or experiences you are documenting. Their first hand accounts add a personal touch and authenticity to your scrapbook.

You can capture detailed stories, emotions, and perspectives that might be missed by traditional journaling. The inclusion of quotes and anecdotes can enrich the narratives and make your scrapbook more engaging.

Different perspectives

If you interview more than one person from an event or occasion, you can include a variety of voices and perspectives in your scrapbook. This diversity adds depth and richness to the overall storytelling.

The spoken or written words of your interviewees provide a lasting record of their experiences, ensuring that important details are not forgotten over time.

Each person you talk to brings their own unique perspective to the story adding complexity and nuance to your scrapbook.

More techniques - Interviews

Here are some ideas to try

Here are some ideas to help you incorporate interviews into your scrapbooking.

Who to interview
Select individuals who are featured in your photos whose perspectives and stories you want to capture.

What to ask
List thoughtful and open-ended questions (ones that require more than a yes or no answer). Tailor questions based on the person's relationship to the event or the theme of your scrapbook.

Set up
Schedule time with your interviewees. Conduct the interviews in person, over the phone, or through written correspondence. Take detailed notes during the interviews or use a recording device if the interviewee is comfortable with it. Ensure that you capture the essence of their stories, emotions, and memories.

Find the highlights
Select key quotes from the interviews that resonate with the theme or message you want to convey in your scrapbook. These quotes can serve as powerful captions or journal entries.

Create Interview Cards
Design cards or tags featuring interview snippets. Attach these to the scrapbook pages for an interactive element. This allows readers to engage directly with the interview content.

Digital Scrapbooking
If you're creating a digital scrapbook, you can embed audio clips, incorporate video snippets, via a QR code.

More techniques - Gratitude Journalling

The idea of this type of journalling is to express gratitude for the people or experiences depicted in the photos, rather than just write about the event, and the things that happened.

Take time to reflect.

Write down few things from your scrapbook layout that you are thankful for.

These could be big or small, ranging from personal achievements and relationships to simple pleasures or moments of joy. The goal is to focus on what is positive and enriching.

Benefits to you

This style of journalling is associated with benefits including improved mental well-being, increased life satisfaction, and reduced stress levels. By shifting our focus from mere events to the underlying moments within them, we open ourselves up to a different view and reading experience for our viewers.

How to do it

As you sit down with your scrapbook layout, take a moment to immerse yourself in the memories captured within it.

Allow yourself to feel the warmth and joy that those experiences brought you. Then jot down a few things that you are thankful for.

These could be significant milestones and cherished relationships to simple delights and fleeting instances of happiness.

Embrace the diversity of positives in your life, both big and small, for they all contribute to your life from year to year.

More techniques - Gratitude Journalling

Try these ideas:

- Express appreciation for the people featured in the photos.

- Share specific qualities or actions you appreciate about each person.

- Reflect on how these individuals have positively impacted your life.

- Discuss the memories or moments you cherish with thanks.

- Explain how the photos serve as reminders of the positive aspects in your life.

- Share any personal anecdotes or stories.

- As you look at the photos, reflect on the qualities and actions that make each individual special to you.

- Consider how people featured in your layouts have contributed positively to your life and the precious memories you hold of them.

- These photos serve as more than just images; they are reminders of the joy and connection you have experienced with each person. Let them bring to mind the happy times, the challenges overcome together.

- Feel free to share personal anecdotes or stories tied to these photos if you feel comfortable to do so. You could always opt for hidden journalling for private reading only.

- Think about the unique qualities and actions of each individual that you deeply appreciate, and the positive influence these individuals have had on your life and the memories you hold dear because of them.

More techniques - Short Captions

If you feel daunted by writing long sections of journalling, there are no rules that say this is how you have to do it. As an alternative to writing paragraphs write short captions for each photo.

Highlight key details or funny anecdotes for each individual picture, building up a written record of your pages, without the need for long sections of prose.

Short captions allow you to convey information in a concise manner. This is important in a visual medium like a scrapbook, where the focus is on the images.

By using short captions for each photo in your scrapbook, you can effectively convey information in a concise manner while highlighting key details or funny anecdotes.

This approach offers a unique way to build up a written record of your pages without the need for lengthy prose.

Each caption acts as a window into the moment captured in the photo, allowing viewers to connect with the story behind the image in a quick and meaningful way.

Using this method allows you to infuse personality and charm into your scrapbook, capturing the essence of each moment with a sprinkling of words.

There are no rules when it comes to creative expression, so feel free to experiment and have fun with your captions!

More techniques - Short Captions

Try these ideas:

- Write a brief caption for each photo, summarizing its significance.
- Describe any humorous or memorable moments associated with the images.
- Explain the relationship between the photos and their chronological order.
- Share any surprising details that might not be immediately apparent in the pictures.
- Highlight the personalities or characteristics of the individuals in the photos.

- Use captions to narrate the photos in a coherent order, numbering if necessary.
- Distribute the short captions evenly across the page, ensuring a balanced look. This helps guide the viewer's eyes smoothly from one photo to the next.
- Add captions that provide context for the location or setting of the photos.
- Ensure that the short captions collectively tell a cohesive story. The captions should work together to enhance the viewer's understanding and emotional connection to the photos.

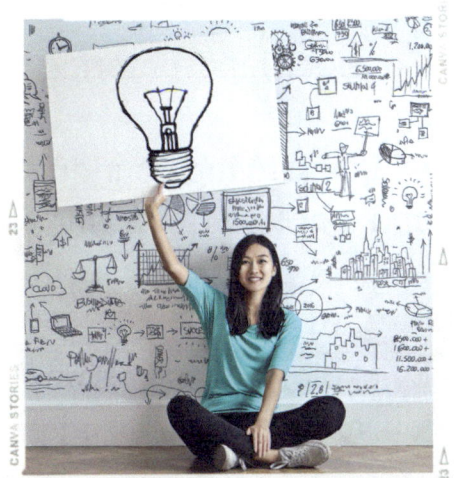

More techniques - Question Prompts

If you are stuck about what to write, having a library of question prompts provides a starting point for your writing. They can spark ideas and provide direction for your journaling and encourage deeper thinking and reflection.

If you're creating a themed scrapbook or want to maintain a consistent tone throughout your journaling, question prompts can help ensure that each entry addresses specific aspects or topics.

Storytelling Questions can guide you in telling a story or sharing specific details about an event, experience, or moment captured in the scrapbook.

Using a variety of question prompts can add diversity to your journaling. This ensures that each entry provides a different perspective or focuses on different aspects of the memories you are capturing.

Consider incorporating questions that spark creativity and encourage reflection.

By diversifying your question prompts, you can delve deeper into your memories and emotions, allowing for a more comprehensive and meaningful scrapbook page.

By exploring various angles and aspects of your memories, you can enrich your journaling journey and uncover new insights and emotions along the way.

Remember, the goal is to craft a meaningful and comprehensive narrative that captures the essence of your experiences. So experiment with different question prompts to ring the changes.

More techniques - Question Prompts

"**Here's some examples:**

- I'll never forget the moment when..."

- "The best part of this day was..."

- "I felt so happy when..."

- "One thing that surprised me during this event was..."

- "I wish I could go back to that day and..."

- "This memory is precious to me because..."

- "If I could relive this moment, I would..."

- "The people involved in this event made it unforgettable by..."

- "I laughed when..."

- "When I look at this layout, I'm reminded of..."

- What events led up to this moment.

- What are the most vivid memories associated with this photo/event?

- Describe the sights, sounds, and smells of the moment.

- Who was with you during this moment, and what role did they play?

- What do you appreciate most about the people involved?

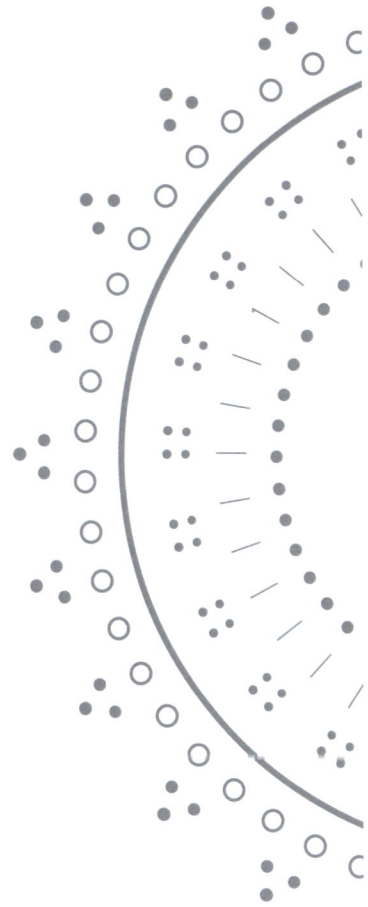

Journalling Prompt Templates

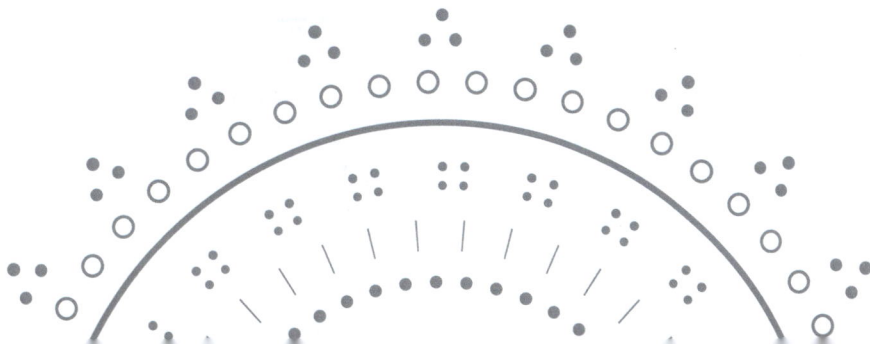

Journalling Prompts

General Page Journalling prompts

☐ Whats the date of this event / photos

☐ Where is it taking place

☐ Who's in the photos and their relationship to you

☐ What is going on / whats the event

☐ Stories that you can't tell by looking at the photos

☐ Something notable or funny that happened

☐ Who said what

☐ Why did you choose that activitiy / place to visit / location / type of event

☐ Five / ten memorable moments list

☐ Interesting things that only people that were there would know

☐ What you felt about the day / your emotions

☐ Add context to daily life - whats in the news at the moment, price of things etc

☐ Ask others that feature to write their thoughts down / ask them for their comments

Journalling Prompts

Book of me (and ideas for photos)

☐ Ten things about me

☐ My favourite recipes

☐ My friends

☐ About my hobbies

☐ A day in my life

☐ My school life

☐ Favourites (Films, music, clothes, places, shops, food etc)

☐ Where have you lived

☐ Five / ten memorable moments list

☐ My family / friends

☐ Whats in my bag

☐ Daily essentials I couldn't live without

☐ Firsts (job, car, holiday etc)

Journalling Prompts

People you scrapbook (son, daughter, friends etc)

☐ Ten things about them
_____

☐ Their proudest acheivements in life / this year / 10 years
_____

☐ What I love about....
_____

☐ About their hobbies
_____

☐ Their work life / school life
_____

☐ How they make you smile / laugh
_____

☐ Favourite activities you do together
_____

☐ How you felt when you met them for the first time
_____

☐ Five / ten memorable moments list
_____

☐ What habits do they have
_____

☐ How they inspire you
_____

☐ What diference have they made to your life
_____

☐ Their favourites (music, films, food, drinks, places to go etc)
_____

Journalling Prompts

Christmas Journalling prompts (and ideas for photos!)

- [ ] Write about your preparations

- [ ] What did you have to eat and who cooked it

- [ ] Who visited or where did you go

- [ ] What Christmas activities to you do every year / Christmas traditions

- [ ] Who do you decorate the house / do you have decorations with special meanings

- [ ] Favourite Christmas memories from your childhood

- [ ] What do you do Christmas eve

- [ ] What gifts do you give and why

- [ ] Five / ten memorable moments list

- [ ] Favourite Christmas Tv programmes / films

- [ ] Christmas Recipes

- [ ] Best memories from this year

- [ ] Ask others that feature to write their thoughts down / ask them for their comments

Journalling Prompts

Holiday (vacation)

- [ ] Write about your preparations and the anticipation of the trip

- [ ] How did you choose where to go

- [ ] Who travelled with you

- [ ] What was the journey like / how did you get there

- [ ] Decribe your holiday home / hotel

- [ ] Talk about the local food / what are your preferred dishes or things you don't like

- [ ] Describe places you visit, memorable experiences, views or places

- [ ] Talk about people you met while travelling and why you remember them

- [ ] Five / ten memorable moments list

- [ ] What did you do for the first time on this holiday

- [ ] Write a travel review - would you return and why

- [ ] Write a 'postcard' home each day of your trip (you could use a notebook for this)

- [ ] Ask others that feature to write their thoughts down / ask them for their comments

Journalling Prompts

Questions about holidays you've taken

- [ ] In your chilldhood, where did you travel to with your family
- [ ] Did your family have a car when you went on holiday as a child - what was it
- [ ] Whats your earliest holiday memory
- [ ] What type of holiday do you prefer
- [ ] Staycation or travel abroad
- [ ] Where do you like to go for your holidays
- [ ] Beach or sightseeing
- [ ] Whats your favourite part of travel
- [ ] How old where you when you got a passport
- [ ] How many countries have you visited - which ones
- [ ] Chilling out or all action
- [ ] What are your favourite dishes from holidays - do you cook them at home
- [ ] How many different types of transport have you used for holidays - what are they

Journalling Prompts

Memories of childhood

☐   Where were you born

☐   What's your earliest memory

☐   What do you remember about your childhood home

☐   What was your fathers' job

☐   What was your mothers' job

☐   What memories do you have of visiting your grandparents

☐   Where did your grandparents live

☐   Where did you go on holiday as a child

☐   What did you enjoy most about childhood holidays

☐   Where did you go to school

☐   What were your favourite school subjects

☐   What childhood games did you play

☐   What hobbies did you have when you were younger that you don't do now

---

Journalling Prompts

☐ What were your favourite childhood TV programmes

☐ Who was your best friend at school

☐ What do you remember about pets you had as a child

☐ What significant news events do you remember from your childhood

☐ What childhood sweets did you like

☐ Who taught you to cook/sew/garden/drive/play an instrument etc etc

☐ Your favourite childhood food

☐ What music did you enjoy as a teenager

☐ Did you earn any badges in Scouts/guides etc

☐ Any awards or prizes you gained as a child

☐ What toys do you remember playing with

☐ Your favourite memory of family celebrations

☐ What did you want to be when you grew up

☐ Did you have a job as a teen - what was it

☐ What was your favourite childhood food

Journalling Prompts

Questions to ask your parents / or yourself!

☐ What is your earliest childhood memory?

☐ Can you share a story or an experience that had a significant impact on your life?

☐ How did you meet each other and fall in love?

☐ What were your dreams and aspirations when you were younger?

☐ What are some of your favorite family traditions or rituals? Why?

☐ What are the most valuable life lessons you've learned

☐ Describe your favorite family trips. What made them special?

☐ Reflect on your career journey. How did you choose your job/profession?

☐ Share a favorite family recipe and the story behind it. Why is it special to you?

☐ Describe a favorite hobby or passion that brings you joy

☐ Describe a person(s) who has had a major influence on your life

☐ Share a family tradition that has been passed down through generations

☐ How many places/houses have your lived in and where were they?

Journalling Prompts

Questions for your children - repeat yearly

☐ How old are you

_____

☐ What school do you go to

_____

☐ What do you enjoy best about school

_____

☐ What don't you like about school

_____

☐ Who is your best friend

_____

☐ What pets do you have

_____

☐ Whats your favourite thing to do

_____

☐ Whats your favourite TV programme

_____

☐ What do you like to play

_____

☐ What food do you like to eat

_____

☐ How much pocket money do you get

_____

☐ What makes you happy

_____

☐ What music / songs do you like

_____

Journalling Prompts

Achievements

☐ Your proudest life achievements so far?

☐ How did you overcome challenges on your journey to achieving your goals?

☐ Were there specific people who played a crucial role in your achievements?

☐ What motivated or inspired you to pursue the goals that you've achieved?

☐ Are there any specific skills or qualities that contributed to your success?

☐ Is there anything you would have done differently on your journey?

☐ How do you set and prioritize goals in your life?

☐ Have you faced any setbacks, and if so, how did you bounce back from them?

☐ What advice would you give to someone?

☐ What advice would you give to your younger self?

☐ Are there any experiences that have shaped your values and principles?

☐ What have working towards, and reaching your goals taught you along the way

☐ What is your next project or goal?

Journalling Prompts

Family

- [ ] Write about your family background and upbringing.

- [ ] What are some of your favourite family traditions?

- [ ] Introduce the members of your immediate family and describe them

- [ ] What roles do you and your family members play in your household?

- [ ] Do you have any family pet names or nicknames?

- [ ] Write about your extended family

- [ ] How often do you spend time with your extended family?

- [ ] What are some of the proudest your family has celebrated?

- [ ] Write about your family's home town

- [ ] Write about the four-legged or furry members of your family.

- [ ] What's your ideal family holiday

- [ ] Write about previous family holidays and what made them memorable.

- [ ] Write about family recipes or traditional food rituals that have been passed down

Journalling Prompts

Friendships

☐ Who is your best friend?

☐ What makes that friendship special?

☐ How did you meet them?

☐ Who are your circle friends, and how did you meet them?

☐ Are there any memorable stories behind your friendships?

☐ What do you like to do when meeting up with friends.

☐ Have you celebrated any significant milestones or life events with your friends?

☐ Is there anything specific you appreciate about each friend?

☐ How do your friends bring out the best in you?

☐ What hobbies and pastimes do you enjoy together?

☐ Who is your longest friend and where did you meet them?

☐ Memories of friends from the past you have lost touch with

☐ Memories about your friends that make your smile.

Journalling Prompts

Partner

- [ ] How did you meet your partner?

- [ ] What attracted you to your partner?

- [ ] What little quirks about them do you love?

- [ ] What are the qualities you most appreciate in your partner?

- [ ] Can you describe your their personality?

- [ ] Are there specific talents or skills your they possesses that you admire?

- [ ] Talk about their hobbies

- [ ] Are there any traditions or routines that are special to your relationship?

- [ ] How do you celebrate birthdays, anniversaries, or other special occasions?

- [ ] What food do they love?

- [ ] What are their top 10 favourite films?

- [ ] Write about their work, what they do and their aspirations for their work.

- [ ] What's on their bucket list?

Journalling Prompts

Travel - talking about your trip

☐ Where did you go?

_____

☐ How did you decide on this particular destination?

_____

☐ How did you plan for your trip?

_____

☐ How did you get to your destination?

_____

☐ Where did you stay?

_____

☐ Memorable people you met on your journey?

_____

☐ What local foods were your favourites?

_____

☐ Did you try any unique or adventurous activities?

_____

☐ Can you recall any specific moments that stood out during your trip?

_____

☐ What was your favourite part of the trip?

_____

☐ Were there any challenges you faced during the trip?

_____

☐ What was your budget, and did you keep to it?

_____

☐ Did it meet your expectations, or did it turn out differently?

_____

Hobbies and Interests

☐ What are your primary hobbies or interests?

_____

☐ Why do you find this hobby so enjoyable?

_____

☐ Have your hobbies changed or evolved over time? If so, how?

_____

☐ Do you have any specific goals or achievements that you're working towards?

_____

☐ Are there any role models or inspirations within your hobby or interest?

_____

☐ What kind of resources or tools do you use to pursue your hobbies?

_____

☐ Write about any meetings, groups or clubs you go to that are related to your hobby.

_____

☐ Have you ever introduced someone else to your hobby? How did they react?

_____

☐ If you could dedicate more time or resources to your hobbies, what would you do?

_____

☐ What disciplines or skills have you learnt to enable you to do your hobby well.

_____

☐ Write about any awards or prizes you have gained as part of your hobby.

_____

☐ What makes you happy about what you do and why?

_____

☐ Can you imagine your life without these hobbies? How would it be different?

_____

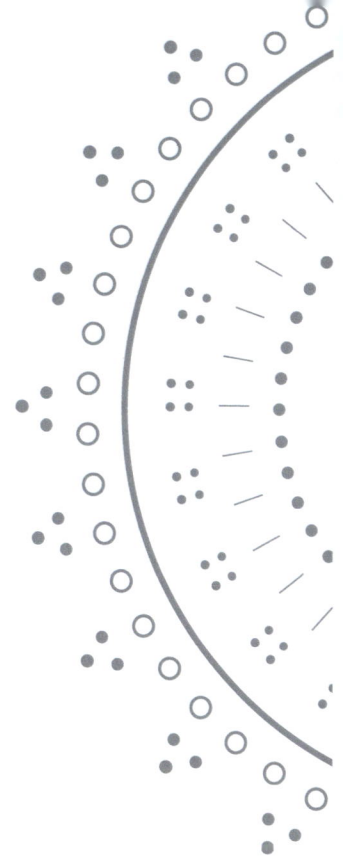

Journalling Prompts

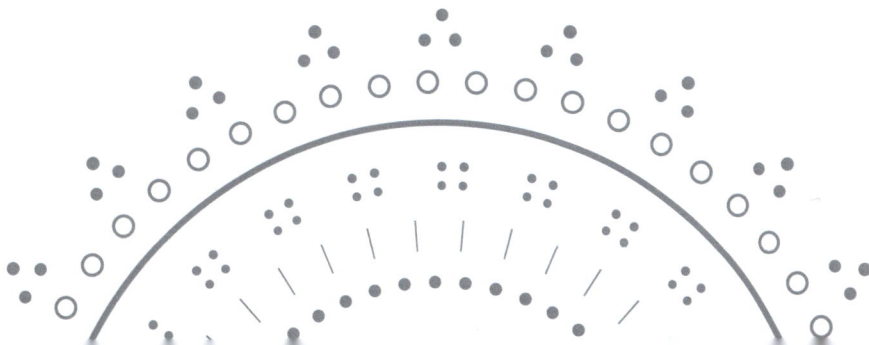

Journalling Prompts

Write your own here:

- [ ] _____
- [ ] _____
- [ ] _____
- [ ] _____
- [ ] _____
- [ ] _____
- [ ] _____
- [ ] _____
- [ ] _____
- [ ] _____
- [ ] _____
- [ ] _____

Journalling Prompts

Write your own here:

- [ ]
- [ ]
- [ ]
- [ ]
- [ ]
- [ ]
- [ ]
- [ ]
- [ ]
- [ ]
- [ ]
- [ ]

Journalling Prompts

Write your own here:

- [ ]
  _____
- [ ]
  _____
- [ ]
  _____
- [ ]
  _____
- [ ]
  _____
- [ ]
  _____
- [ ]
  _____
- [ ]
  _____
- [ ]
  _____
- [ ]
  _____
- [ ]
  _____
- [ ]
  _____

Journalling Prompts

Write your own here:

- [ ] _____
- [ ] _____
- [ ] _____
- [ ] _____
- [ ] _____
- [ ] _____
- [ ] _____
- [ ] _____
- [ ] _____
- [ ] _____
- [ ] _____
- [ ] _____

Journalling Prompts

Write your own here:

- ☐ _____
- ☐ _____
- ☐ _____
- ☐ _____
- ☐ _____
- ☐ _____
- ☐ _____
- ☐ _____
- ☐ _____
- ☐ _____
- ☐ _____
- ☐ _____

Journalling Prompts

Write your own here:

- [ ] _____
- [ ] _____
- [ ] _____
- [ ] _____
- [ ] _____
- [ ] _____
- [ ] _____
- [ ] _____
- [ ] _____
- [ ] _____
- [ ] _____
- [ ] _____

Journalling Prompts

Write your own here:

- [ ]
- [ ]
- [ ]
- [ ]
- [ ]
- [ ]
- [ ]
- [ ]
- [ ]
- [ ]
- [ ]
- [ ]

Journalling Prompts

Write your own here:

- [ ] _____
- [ ] _____
- [ ] _____
- [ ] _____
- [ ] _____
- [ ] _____
- [ ] _____
- [ ] _____
- [ ] _____
- [ ] _____
- [ ] _____
- [ ] _____

The Weekly Sketch

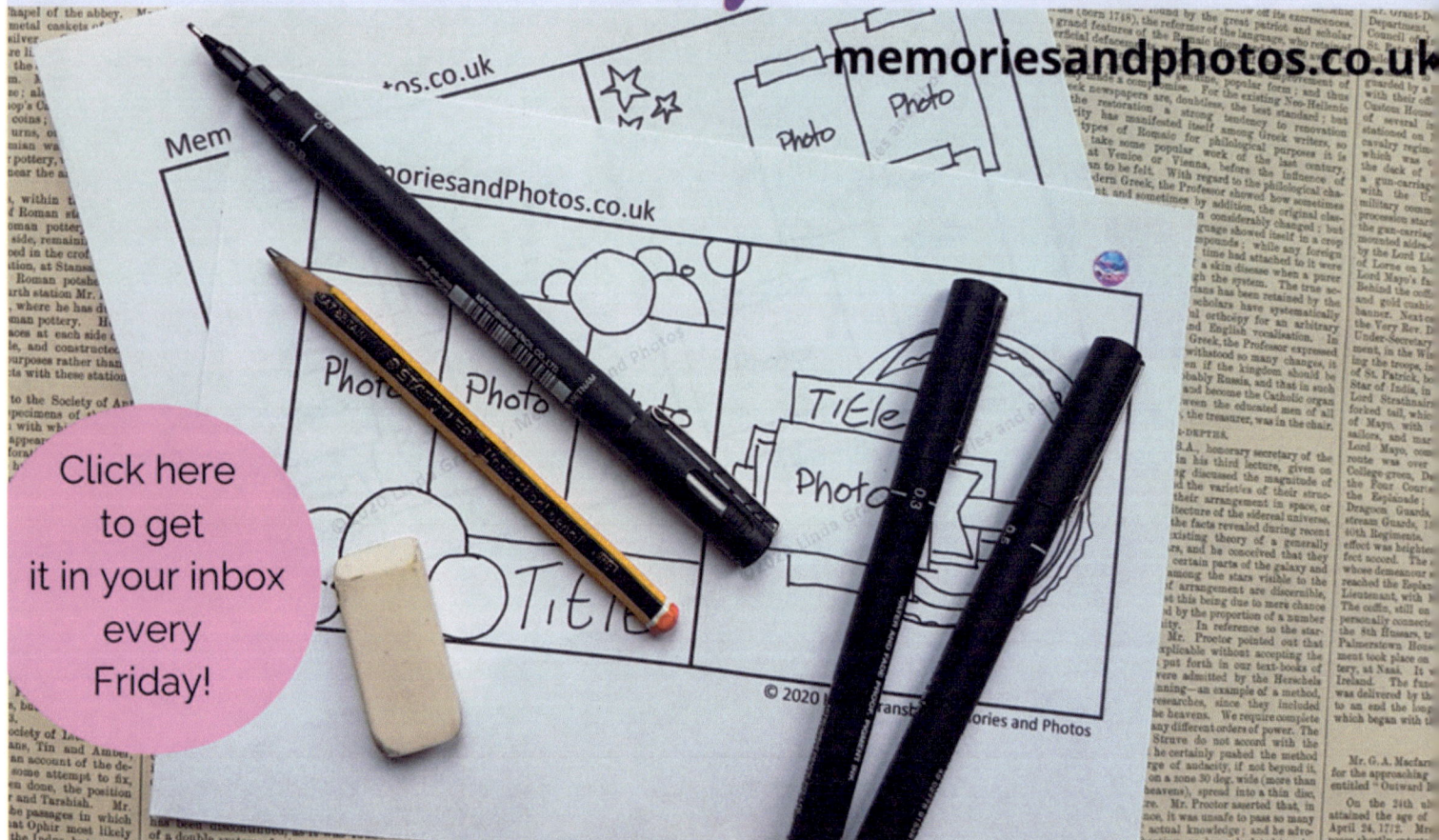

memoriesandphotos.co.uk

Click here to get it in your inbox every Friday!

Want more inspiration?

Have you had a day when you sit looking at your supplies and photos and don't know what to do or where to start.....? That's what inspired me to create The Weekly Sketch.

Page layout ideas to get your mojo going!

You can get the weekly sketch in your inbox every week for free.... just click here or scan the QR code

https://bit.ly/weeklysketch

Linda x

Journalling Prompts

Write your own here:

- [ ]
- [ ]
- [ ]
- [ ]
- [ ]
- [ ]
- [ ]
- [ ]
- [ ]
- [ ]
- [ ]
- [ ]

Journalling Prompts

Write your own here:

- [ ] _____
- [ ] _____
- [ ] _____
- [ ] _____
- [ ] _____
- [ ] _____
- [ ] _____
- [ ] _____
- [ ] _____
- [ ] _____
- [ ] _____
- [ ] _____

Journalling Prompts

Write your own here:

- [ ] _____
- [ ] _____
- [ ] _____
- [ ] _____
- [ ] _____
- [ ] _____
- [ ] _____
- [ ] _____
- [ ] _____
- [ ] _____
- [ ] _____
- [ ] _____

Journalling Prompts

Write your own here:

- [ ]
  _____
- [ ]
  _____
- [ ]
  _____
- [ ]
  _____
- [ ]
  _____
- [ ]
  _____
- [ ]
  _____
- [ ]
  _____
- [ ]
  _____
- [ ]
  _____
- [ ]
  _____
- [ ]
  _____

Journalling Prompts

Write your own here:

- [ ] _____
- [ ] _____
- [ ] _____
- [ ] _____
- [ ] _____
- [ ] _____
- [ ] _____
- [ ] _____
- [ ] _____
- [ ] _____
- [ ] _____
- [ ] _____

Hi, I'm Linda

Linda is a passionate crafter, experienced teacher and founder of Memories and Photos. She has over 20 years experience in the crafting world.

Her speciality is providing simple solutions to allow busy people to enjoy their craft time.

Linda runs relaxed, workshop-style country house craft retreats for time starved crafters, and curates the monthly Scrap Box; coordinated supplies for stress-free shopping.

She also designs 'The Weekly Sketch' with simple layouts, page examples and advice to inspire 'stuck' and time starved scrapbookers.

She has published 2 books so far (available on Amazon). Her page designs have been published in Scrapbooking Magazine, and she been a guest writer for 'Your Family History Magazine'.

She has been a featured guest speaker on main stage at craft business conferences a number of times, and has demonstrated at national craft shows.

When you meet her you'll most likely find her with a cuppa in her hand, and barefoot; it helps her create better!

She lives in Bedfordshire, UK and enjoys crafting (of course!) photography, travel and cycling.

Linda@memoriesandphotos.co.uk

@memoriesandphotos.co.uk

Memories and Photos

GOLD STUDENTS' CHOICE AWARD
RATED EXCELLENT ON CRAFTCOURSES.COM

Your Family History

STAMPEROAMA

CREATIVE MEMORIES

BBC THREE COUNTIES RADIO

hobbycraft

Can you help?

Love this book? Can you take 5 mins to leave a review?

Every review matters when you're an independent business!

Head over to Amazon or wherever you purchased this book to leave an honest review for me.

I thank you for your time

Thank You!

Made in United States
Troutdale, OR
02/07/2025